Morocco

EVERGREEN is an imprint of Benedikt Taschen Verlag GmbH

© for this edition: 1998 Benedikt Taschen Verlag GmbH
Hohenzollernring 53, D–50672 Köln
© 1997 Editions du Chêne – Hachette Livre – Le Maroc
Under the direction of Michel Buntz – Hoa Qui Photographic Agency
Editor: Corinne Fossey
Maps and illustrations: Jean-Michel Kirsch
Text: Hugues Demeude
Photographs: Jacques Bravo and Xavier Richer
Cover: Angelika Taschen, Cologne
Translated by Phil Goddard
In association with First Edition Translations Ltd, Cambridge
Realization of the English edition by First Edition Translations Ltd, Cambridge

Printed in Italy
ISBN 3-8228-7757-3

MOROCCO

Text HUGUES DEMEUDE

Photographs JACQUES BRAVO AND XAVIER RICHER

EVERGREEN

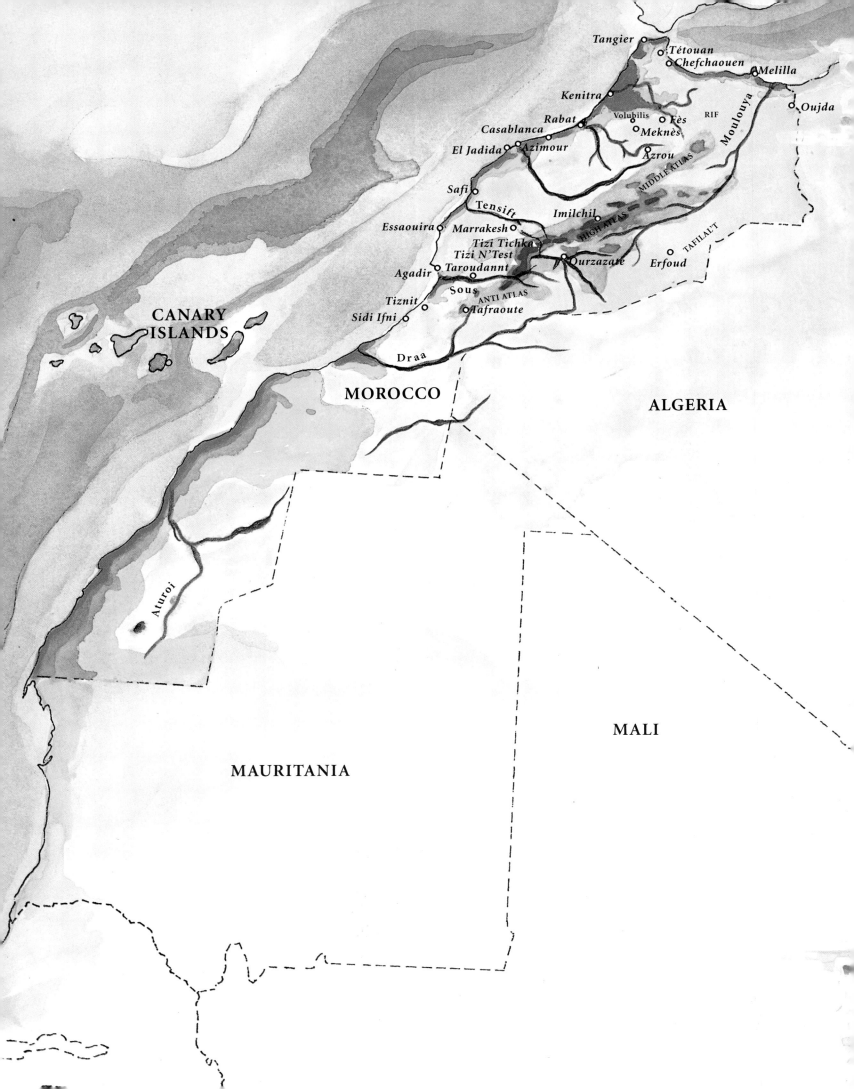

The Kingdom of Morocco is a land of legend, a melting-pot of many different civilizations, and a place of endless mystery. It is home to a blend of cultures, many of whose traditions have survived both the positive and the negative changes wrought by the twentieth century, and the country is a cornucopia for travellers who come to experience its beauty for themselves. More so than in other countries, a complex geographical and geological makeup has resulted in a great variety of landscapes, and Morocco's enigmatic complexity is reflected in the culture of its people.

From the golden beaches of the Atlantic to the steeply rising coasts of the Mediterranean, from arid ranges of snow-capped mountains over 4,000 metres (13,000 ft) high to forests of cedars and vast sandy plains, the landscapes of Morocco are a source of endless wonder for visitors. But perhaps even more importantly, the qualities on which this nation most prides itself are qualities of the heart and the mind. The most fascinating feature of this land is its people, a mixture of Arabs, Berbers, and Saharan nomads who, for all the upheavals they have undergone in recent decades, still seem close to nature, and are still renowned for their generous hospitality. Islam has guided every aspect of their lives for nearly twelve centuries, and Morocco has proved fertile territory for the growth of this religion.

Many visible traces remain of Morocco's history since the first Islamic kingdom was founded here in the eighth century by Idris I. These give some insight into the turbulent events and the artistic creativity that have shaped this country over the span of six dynasties. But the best way of understanding the soul of modern-day Morocco is through contact with the passion and humility displayed by its people.

Muslim geographers from the east called Morocco *Maghreb el-Aqsa*, the country of the far west. They found a place of striking contrasts, of jagged mountain landscapes and plains stretching as far as the eye could see. The country is dominated by the imposing peaks of the High and Middle Atlas mountains; the highest point is Jebel (Mount) Toubkal, 4,167 metres (13,750 ft) above sea level, where skiers can indulge their passion near the village of Oukaimeden. To the north-east, Jebel Ayachi reaches a height of 3,737 metres (12,332 ft). In the north of Morocco, overlooking the Mediterranean, is the legendary Rif, a crescent-shaped mountain chain with Jebel Tidirhine the highest peak at 2,456 metres (8,104 ft). In the south, the harsh plateau of the Anti-Atlas gazes out across the Sahara. Rain and melted snow from these mountains fill the many seasonal watercourses known as wadis, providing irrigation for a 2,500-kilometre (1,600-mile) strip of land along the Atlantic coast, for 500 kilometres (300 miles) beside the Mediterranean, and to a lesser extent for the slopes facing the Sahara.

The soil is surprisingly generous to the people of Morocco. There are woodlands and forests of cedar and oak, as well as oil-bearing argan trees, olives, palms, and orange and almond trees; while the many crops include grapes, maize, barley, wheat, henna, and any number of different vegetables. All are dependent on the Atlas mountains, whose central position helps to give Morocco its feeling of coherence and unity.

In its time, Morocco has been peopled by many races. The first in this long succession were the Berbers, who were later followed by the Phoenicians, the Romans, the Vandals, and the Byzantines. The year 682 marked a crucial milestone in the history of the Moroccan nation, for it was in this year that Oqba Ben Nafi and his army of Muslim Arabs arrived bearing the message of Islam as revealed by the prophet Mohammed. A century later, Idris Ben Abdallah – a descendant of Ali, the prophet's son-in-law – found refuge here and became the first sultan of the Islamic kingdom of Maghreb el-Aqsa.

He helped to spread Islam, which rapidly became the cornerstone of Moroccan unity. Idris was followed by other nobles descended from the prophet Mohammed who founded the Idrisid, Saadian, and Alawi dynasties, as well as the powerful Berber aristocracies represented by the Almoravid, Almohad, and Marinid dynasties.

Overleaf: Taroudannt and the snow-capped Atlas mountains.

7

Over the centuries, they developed a unique culture in which art, architecture, crafts, and life itself were all devoted to the greater glory of God.

Throughout its history, Islam has welded together the different components that make up the Moroccan people, and it is a profoundly tolerant, open, and generous religion. Simplicity, hospitality, and human warmth are the hallmarks of its people: the architect from Casablanca, the goldsmith from Chefchaouen, the fisherman from Essaouira, the Berber shepherd from the High Atlas, the hotel manager from Marrakesh, the Touareg woman from the Sahara. As King Hassan II points out in his book, *The Challenge*: "Morocco is like a tree whose nourishing roots plunge deep into the soil of Africa, and which breathes through its leaves, which rustle in the winds blowing from Europe."

There is much to be gained by understanding and fostering European influences in Morocco. At the end of his book, published in 1976, King Hassan II recalls the words of an Italian expert on Morocco who was a vice-president of the European Commission at the time. "Over and above the many historical, geographical, and trading links between Europe and Morocco, the Mediterranean represents a vitally important region for the European Community. The development of good relations between these coastal nations is essential for the stability and security of all the European Community countries." This comment is just as true now as it was twenty years ago.

Right: Tangier is spread out like an amphitheatre, with the Mediterranean the stage.
Opposite: The Bab Bhar, one of the gates to Africa.

Tangier is a mythical crossroads between Europe and Africa, and a point of convergence between the green waters of the Atlantic and the blue Mediterranean Sea. It is the gateway to Morocco, a legendary stopping-off place for seafarers from all over the world, and a cosmopolitan city that has attracted rootless souls for over a century.

In a book about Tangier published in 1990, it is significant that the French journalist Daniel Rondeau quotes one of the city's most famous residents, the American writer Paul Bowles: "I had always known that one day in my life, I would enter a place which gave me both wisdom and ecstasy." Bowles found this place of revelation in 1931 when he discovered what he called "Tangier the white". The city's history is an eventful one. For the Phoenicians, it was a strategic trading-post in the Straits of Gibraltar; then, for over a century, it was the subject of rivalry between the Idrisids and the Omeyyads of Spain. Tangier was the subject of fierce battles for control by each of the Berber dynasties, and was an international zone between 1923 and 1959.

The city has proved a powerful attraction to travellers from all over the world; in its time, it has been the place where artists have come in search of authentic African experience, a meeting-place for rich eccentrics, and an exciting destination for adventurers of all kinds. As Daniel Rondeau puts it in his book on the city: "For a moment, looking out from the houses on Cap Spartel or the walls of the kasbah, you feel you could almost stretch out an arm and touch Spain. Europe is so close that for years people crossed the strait as though crossing a river in summer, to go and picnic with friends. People came from everywhere: some for a week, some for a month, some for life. Tangier was a pleasure-ground for the dilettantes of the modern world, tinged with melancholy."

Today, the streets of Tangier are no longer filled with the sounds of partygoers, and the city is no longer eyed so covetously by Europeans. But it is still an overpoweringly stimulating place, spread out like an amphitheatre looking out across the Mediterranean, with a large proportion of its 350,000 population enjoying a spectacular panoramic view of the great and tranquil

Above: The Mediterranean expands outwards to the horizon from the heights of the Rif. Opposite: The Mediterranean coast is dotted with small, isolated, and tranquil bays.

Passengers are ferried across the estuary of the Bou Regreg between Rabat and Salé.

bay. A ring of sandy beaches links the mirror-smooth blue sea to the land rising steeply into the city's seven hills, which protect it from the Atlantic winds.

The city has undergone radical change over the past fifty years. Large and imposing buildings have sprung up almost overnight, turning Tangier into a modern seaside metropolis. The Petit Socco – the old souk district in the medina – still fulfils European stereotypes of what such a market should be. It was traditionally the place where goods on their way to and from the port were bought and sold, but today it is surrounded by hotels, banks, and restaurants. A few narrow streets further on, the Place du 9 avril 1947, more commonly known as the Grand Socco, is still vibrant and noisy, the air filled with the laughter and curses of artisans and traders as it has been since time immemorial. This great souk is overlooked by the minaret of the Sidi Bou Abid mosque, with its multicoloured faience tiles. In the market itself, Berber peasant women from the neighbouring Rif mountains, dressed in the traditional red and white striped lengths of cloth known as foutas, and in hats with

blue pompons, sell a huge variety of fruit, fabrics, and baskets. The air is filled with strong, acrid smells and subtle perfumes. Many aspects of people's daily lives have changed little over the centuries. The medina of Tangier is also famous for its kasbah, containing the sultan's palace, the Dar el-Makhzen. Begun by Sultan Moulay Ismail in the late seventeenth century, this fortress is a reminder both of the simple, harsh existence of the time when it was built, and of the highly sophisticated architecture and crafts which were available to those who could afford them. The palace's marble columns, cedarwood ceilings, and decorated arches are now the home of the Museum of Antiquities and the Museum of Moroccan Art, providing an insight into a world which was normally hidden from the view of most people.

Rabat is an extraordinary city in an extraordinary country. It is Morocco's second largest inhabited area, with a population of nearly a million; it is also the administrative capital, the seat of government, and the focus of royal authority. It is the best maintained of all Moroccan cities, the greenest, and the most prosperous; in some

Top: A Rabat boatman in traditional costume steers his way across the Bou Regreg, which flows into the Atlantic Ocean.
Above: Rabat's famous Kasbah des Oudaïa seen from the ancient town of Salé.
Overleaf: The royal burial ground of Chellah, with its powerful ramparts, is one of Rabat's best-known landmarks.

This gate in the walls surrounding the Kasbah des Oudaia leads to a museum and a garden, both very popular with the people of Rabat.

places it looks almost wealthy, particularly the Avenue Mohamed V between the Great Mosque and the ministry district, near the Royal Palace.

There is a strong European influence, but this does not detract at all from the charm of Rabat. The five main features that together constituted the entire city at the beginning of the century have been well preserved: the medina, winding its way along between the ocean and the Bou Regreg river; the Kasbah des Oudaia; the Royal Palace; the royal burial ground of Chellah; and the old town of Salé on the other side of the river.

The Kasbah des Oudaia dates back to the period during which the Almohad sultan Yacoub el-Mansour made the city his capital. In the twelfth century, he built this fortress above the port to protect the estuary from possible attack. It went on to become a powerful military and administrative area, and the magnificent Porte des Oudaia (the Oudaia being the descendants of the redoubtable Arab warriors who rebelled against the sherif sultans) is one of the finest of all examples of Almohad art.

Rabat's medina is smaller and more modern than those of Marrakesh and Fès. But it has the same narrow, meandering streets, the same frenetic bustle, and the same smells that the French resident-general, General Lyautey, would have experienced in 1912, when he decided to make Rabat the administrative centre of the French protectorate and banned any further building within the walls of the medina.

Since then, nestling between the Almohad and Andalusian walls, it has provided a means of access from the estuary to the port.

Rabat's two most famous monuments, the Tour Hassan and the mausoleum of Mohamed V, are in the "new" part of the city, along an esplanade that symbolizes Morocco's pride in its independence. The 44-metre (145-ft) Tour Hassan stands silhouetted against the city when viewed from the west, and was once the minaret of the great mosque built by Yacoub el-Mansour. Its lozenge-shaped tracery and trefoil arches are typical of Almohad architecture, recalling the Koutoubia Mosque in Marrakesh and creating the same feeling of solidity and majesty. Opposite this important

A silver door knocker depicting the hand of Fatima, the daughter of the prophet Mohammed; this is intended to bring good luck and ward off the evil eye.

Left and opposite: Rabat's medina is famous for its white walls and beautifully coloured doors. Each household vies constantly with its neighbours for the best-decorated and best-maintained door. Overleaf: The Feast of the Throne, held on 3 March each year, commemorates the accession of King Hassan II. Local leaders from all over the country gather for the two-day event.

structure is the mausoleum of Mohamed V, the great Alawi sultan who died five years after obtaining his country's independence in 1956. It is a masterpiece of Moroccan craftsmanship.

Reflecting the respect in which the figure of the king is still held, all of the buildings housing the mausoleum are richly decorated. Their sculpted wood and marble, the bright red, black, and green mosaic friezes known as zelliges, and the carved bronze and stained-glass windows create an atmosphere of contemplation and repose.

But the real architectural focus of Rabat lies to the south. The Royal Palace is a veritable city within a city, built at the end of an impressive mechouar, a large square which was a traditional tribal meeting-place during festivals. When the king is in residence in Rabat, it is sometimes possible to see him and his retinue crossing the esplanade to the El-Faeh Mosque at prayer time on Friday at 12.30. It is a solemn and majestic procession, evoking the power of tradition, the intense faith of the believers, and the important role which the king still plays in their lives.

The country's only major highway links Rabat, Morocco's

The tomb of Mohamed V is an important place of pilgrimage and a jewel of Islamic art. Its architecture, and its sculpted wood and metal and faience mosaics in geometric patterns, invite contemplation.

The Hassan II Mosque is the biggest place of prayer in the Muslim world after Mecca. It is a gigantic and powerful building, with a minaret 200 metres (660 ft) high. The mosque was built by some 10,000 master craftsmen and apprentices, and is a monument of great artistic splendour.

administrative and diplomatic capital, with Casablanca, the busy trading port which acts as a magnet for the richest and poorest people in the country.

The road runs along the coast, and has greatly reduced the travelling time between those two important centres of power. Casablanca is expanding at an ever-increasing rate. At the beginning of the century, it was only a small town which had grown up from nothing. Since then, Casa, as it is known, has gradually become a huge, sprawling metropolis with an official population of four million and an actual population which is probably larger. It is now the fourth biggest city in Africa after Cairo, Alexandria, and Lagos, and people are still descending on it in great numbers from the poorer parts of Morocco to find work, which is in short supply elsewhere. As a result, the city continues to expand in every direction, and the streets grow ever more crowded during the day. But it is still a place of boundless energy and hope, and like so many cities whose streets are supposedly paved with gold, it is a place of striking contrast between wealth and poverty. The opulent splendour of some of its

This page: Many fountains are decorated using the typical cutout ceramic panels known as zelliges. Opposite: The spacious harmony of the Hassan II Mosque.

more affluent suburbs makes Beverly Hills look down-at-heel by comparison, and even the poorest districts are full of life and colour. In the space of a few minutes, you will see descendants of leading families from Fès and Marrakesh who have started their own businesses here, as well as elderly property developers and youthful stock-exchange traders. But you will also see the old men in the medina, the children cleaning shoes, and the Berber peasants from the distant Atlas mountains living in exile here and trying to earn a crust. The two groups may rub shoulders in the crowded streets, but they live in two different worlds.

Casablanca is a western-style city. The centre, with its skyscraper apartment and office blocks, its wide boulevards jammed solid with cars, and its large gardens and spacious esplanades, is the fruit of western city planning. The area where the main street joins the

*W*omen, *their beauty veiled in the traditional costume of Essaouira,*
deep in discussion beneath the walls of the town.
The pink ramparts of Essaouira are made from a local material.

• Essaouira, the "well designed" •

The narrow peninsula on which Essaouira stands is an ancient site which was well known to Phoenician merchants and to the Romans. But it was not until 1765 that the Alawi sultan Mohamed ben Abdallah ordered the changes which resulted in Essaouira becoming known as the "well-designed city" or the "St-Malo of Africa". At the beginning of the sixteenth century, the Portuguese had built a small port and a fortress on this site, which was known as Mogador. After the Saadians regained possession of it, the Alawi sultan was determined to turn it into a port to rival Agadir, which was rebelling against central government. He ordered a captured French architect, Théodore Cornut, to carry out this work, and Cornut designed and built the first port and the kasbah. The sqala of the kasbah, with its large number of cannons, the medina, the mellah or Jewish quarter, and the ramparts (which are still there today) were built shortly afterwards.

Previous page: The walls of Essaouira look down on the pounding breakers of the Atlantic.

Boulevard Roudani, next to the new Twin Center office block, has been called the Champs-Elysées of Casablanca because of its high concentration of fashionable shops, restaurants, bars, and department stores. Further on, past the Parc de la Ligue Arabe, the Place des Nations-Unies forms the administrative centre of the city.

The kasbah is surrounded by magnificent ochre-coloured buildings. The Palais de Justice and the prefecture overlook an immense boulevard which is always thronged with people, and from here there is a superb view of the sunset, with the pinkish-bronze light bringing a deep glow to the walls of the buildings. As you continue along the Avenue Hassan II towards the port, the numerous avenues and boulevards leading off the Place Mohamed V make it the city's busiest crossroads. The nearby ancient medina, like those in other Moroccan cities, is a labyrinth of open, narrow streets crowded with all kinds of shops and small businesses. Snack stalls, restaurants, and sellers of household utensils, clothes, and tobacco compete for the attention of the crowds of passers-by who fill the streets of the medina.

Beyond the port, which forms a large extension to the old nucleus of Casablanca along the ocean to the south, is the formidable Hassan II Mosque. This was inaugurated on 30 August 1993, and marks the westernmost outpost of Islam; after Mecca, it is the biggest place of worship in the Muslim world. The mosque is a gigantic, majestic building with a minaret 200 metres (650 ft) high. Its prayer hall is 20,000 square metres (216,000 sq ft) in area, with space for up to 25,000 worshippers, and its esplanade holds up to 80,000 people. The mosque was paid for by contributions from every Moroccan citizen, and thus symbolizes the unity of the nation and its people. It also shows that traditional Moroccan craftsmanship is alive and well: some 10,000 master craftsmen and apprentices were involved in constructing and decorating the building.

The corniche of Casablanca, further to the south, is home to countless public baths, smart restaurants, nightclubs, and even a jazz bar. At night, when the streets of central Casablanca are deserted and

families are spending time together at home, this area pulsates with the kind of night-time pleasures which Europeans take for granted, but which have little place in the Muslim world.

A beautiful 350-kilometre (218-mile) coast road runs from Casablanca to the stunning little town of Essaouira. There are a number of towns along the way which are worth an extended visit, the first of which is Azemmour. Despite being no great distance from Casablanca, it is a perfect example of an authentic Moroccan town, with whitewashed houses, ochre-coloured ramparts, and gardens full of flowers. It is also a place of tranquillity after the hubbub of the big city. Located on the edge of the ocean and at the mouth of the Oum er-Rbia river, it has a pleasant climate and the unhurried pace of what is predominantly an agricultural town.

Further along the road, on the other side of the river, is the former Portuguese town of El Jadida. The town is full of history, and its fast-expanding population of 150,000 means that it is well on the way to becoming an important local centre. Founded by the Portuguese as a trading centre early in the sixteenth century, El

Above right: The walls of the former medina are white, the doors and windows blue.
Above left: Portuguese cannon lined up along the ramparts, with the sqala of the kasbah visible in the distance.

*A*bove *and opposite: The port of Essaouira is well known as a centre for building and maintaining trawlers.*
Overleaf: The red earth of the Safi region, on the Atlantic coast.

Jadida still bears the traces of the turbulent period when it was fought over by the Portuguese and the sultans of the Alawi dynasty. Hence the ramparts, and in particular the two fortresses of St Sebastian and the Angel, which provide a permanent reminder of the vicious wars being fought when they were built. Today, El Jadida's beach, and its newly built port, have provided it with more peaceful ways of earning a livelihood.

The next stop along the coast road is the attractive little town of Oualidia, followed in turn by Safi, which has a rather more tempestuous history. It is one of Morocco's leading ports, and is well known for its important sardine-fishing industry and for

Safi is known throughout Morocco for its shiny glazed pottery.
Most households own at least one piece.

• Safi and its pottery •

Safi pottery is very popular in Morocco. Legend has it that some potters from Fès were passing through the Safi area, and found the local clay to be of such high quality that they decided to settle in the town and make pottery there.

The industry is still thriving today, and there are around a hundred potters' kilns clustered on one hill in the town. The potters' quarter, on the side of this hill, is full of shops where you can buy finely decorated, brightly coloured glazed plates, bowls, and traditional containers known as tajines. The potters have formed a co-operative and set up a school to pass their skills on to future generations.

phosphate production; the main reason for stopping here is the old quarter. A much more attractive place, some 100 kilometres (60 miles) to the south, is the town of Essaouira. Essaouira is a resting-place for the traveller, an oasis of coolness. This compact walled town is entirely blue and white; its house-fronts are whitewashed, and its doors and windows are painted in various shades of blue. The heat of the reflected sun is tempered by cooling sea breezes.

Because it was so well protected and able to accommodate so many ships, the port of Essaouira soon became one of the principal destinations of camel caravans from the Sahara, laden with gold, ivory, ebony, salt, ostrich feathers, and slaves. These were exchanged for produce from Europe, such as cotton goods, spices, and tobacco. The town became such an important trading centre that by the beginning of the nineteenth century, an estimated 40% of all goods from the Atlantic coast passed through it. Although it may not be quite such a thriving place today, it earns a comfortable enough living from fishing, handicrafts, and tourism, and its old-world

*T*he fortified town of El Jadida
provides many reminders of the
country's turbulent past, and of the
fighting between the Portuguese and
the sultans of the Alawi dynasty.

charm remains unaltered by the years. Much of its attractiveness
derives from its relatively sedate pace, from the nonchalant beauty
of the women, and the friendliness of the men.

Essaouira has always been a very cosmopolitan place, with a population including Arabs, Saharans, Moroccan Jews, and Europeans.
But it is also very much influenced by the distinctively African culture of the gnaoua, a religious brotherhood based on trance music,
ritual possession, and geomancy, in which patterns of earth ran-
domly thrown on the ground are used to divine the future.
Essaouira has also exerted a powerful attraction on Europeans of
an artistic turn of mind: visitors have included the French airman
and author Antoine de Saint-Exupéry, Orson Welles, the abstract
artist Nicolas de Staël, and even Jimi Hendrix – who at one stage
was intent on buying up the entire town. Despite this influx of for-
eigners, however, it has retained much of its mystery.

As you travel south, the landscape changes dramatically just before
Agadir, becoming more rocky and more vividly coloured. Agadir
itself, sprawled out along the plain of the Sous and nestled between

*The Portuguese Cistern, a silent,
mysterious place, is one of El Jadida's
best-known landmarks.*

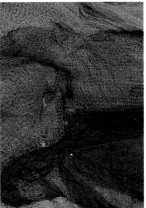

*A*bove and opposite: Fishing-nets
form a brightly coloured carpet in
the port of El Jadida.

the High Atlas and the Anti-Atlas, is Morocco's leading seaside resort. Each year, it plays host to hundreds of thousands of tourists, who come here mainly for its mild climate with 300 days of sunshine, and for its 10 kilometres (6 miles) of irresistible fine sandy beaches. Agadir is a playground set against a deep blue sky and an azure ocean, the ideal place either to sit and do nothing or to sample a wide range of sporting activities.

As well as being a place of relaxation for holidaymakers, Agadir is a busy industrial centre in its own right. It is Morocco's biggest fishing port, and the oil tanks, cement works, and fish-preserving factories in the Anza district of the town are reflections of its rapid

*A*bove: *Behind the seven doors of the Royal Palace in Fès lies a beautiful and secret world. Opposite: One of the earliest fountains in the Old Town of Fès. Overleaf: Fès from the fortress of the Borj Nord.*

economic growth, which has occurred despite the devastating earthquake of 1960 which killed 15,000 people. If Agadir were to have a motto, perhaps it should be the words of King Mohamed V, who said: "It may have been fate that brought about the destruction of Agadir, but rebuilding it is a task which demands faith and willpower on our part."

The Rif is one of Morocco's two great chains of mountains, the other being the Atlas. It runs for some 250 kilometres (160 miles) along the northern coast, rising steeply from the sea, and is 150 kilometres (95 miles) across at its widest point. As a result, northern Morocco is a geographically distinctive region, from its towering mountain summits to the narrow and indented shores of the Mediterranean. The steep slopes of the mountains have been eroded by torrents and heavy winter rains, creating a harsh, wild landscape. Until recently, it was the undisputed province of the Berbers, who were the feared and respected rulers of what was believed to be an inaccessible land.

The road to Chefchaouen, a small town hidden away in the moun-

tains at an altitude of 800 metres (2,600 ft), is a slow and winding one. It is also highly scenic, thanks mainly to the attractive villages which cling to the reddish-brown mountainsides. Along the way you will pass processions of Berber peasants on donkeys, going to market in Tétouan, the women dressed in the typical fouta and pompon hat.

You may also see customs planes looking for people trafficking in kif, which is widely grown in this area. The journey is a gradual acclimatization to the harsh life of the Rif. Then, suddenly, the town of Chefchaouen appears, tucked away in a valley so that its red roofs, white terraces, and Mediterranean-blue doors and windows come into sight at the last minute. Chefchaouen is the kind of town that people take an instant liking to. It spills down the side of the valley, its neatly geometric cube-shaped houses contrasting with its haphazard tangle of narrow streets. The town was founded in 1471 by an Arab prince, Ali Ben Rechid, who left Granada and decided to create a stronghold from which he could launch attacks on Ceuta, which had been captured by the king of Portugal. The

The green roofs of the Qarawiyine University Mosque. Green is a symbolic colour in Islam.

• The restoration of the medina at Fès •

In 1889, the French decadent novelist Pierre Loti wrote of the medina in Fès: "O dark Maghreb, long may you remain immured and impenetrable to everything that is new; turn your back on Europe and immerse yourself in the things of the past." A century later, UNESCO designated the medina a World Heritage Site and began a complete restoration of the old city. The Moroccan government set up a body responsible for restoring around fifty of the most important buildings and a large number of smaller ones; the total cost of this huge project is estimated at $600 million. Maalems – traditional craftsmen – are restoring the original structures and decoration so that future generations will be able to use and enjoy the ancient medina.

*T*his page and opposite: Some of
Fès's medersas, or religious colleges.

kasbah, walls, and ramparts of Chefchaouen are a memorial to its glorious military past. Like Tétouan, the town bears traces of Andalusian influence in its decorative arts. In the past, it was one of Morocco's most flourishing centres of craftsmanship, specializing in iron, leather, and wood. Today, it is still known for its attractive sculptures made from cedar, and its equally eye-catching Berber carpets. Chefchaouen is also a place of remarkable gentleness: the air is steeped in the fragrance of flowers and the sound of trickling water; old women veiled in the traditional haik shuffle laboriously along, and endearingly noisy children chase one another through the back streets. This is a town often described as holy, and it is certainly a place that makes a strong impression.

The succession of mountains beyond Chefchaouen is carpeted with trees: almonds, pines, cork oaks, and especially cedars, which are

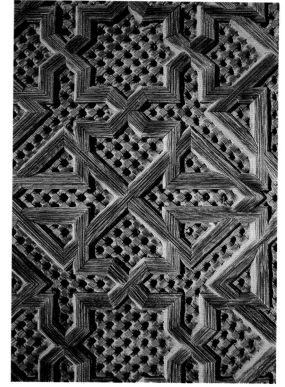

particularly abundant at around 2,000 metres (6,500 ft). There is also a scattering of villages, which are the homes of Berber tribes. The Berbers are mostly farmers, working on the steep mountainsides to produce crops of wheat, maize, hemp, fruit, and vegetables. They are also stock-breeders whose herds of goats and sheep are often their most valuable asset, while hardy donkeys and mules help to take some of the strain out of their arduous existence. The people of the Rif have always been very much a race of mountain-dwellers, and have little interest in the sea or in the scope it offers for earning a living.

Cradled in the lap of this legendary mountain barrier lie the two imperial cities of Meknès and Fès. Meknès is less well known than its very famous neighbour, but is nevertheless sufficiently extraordinary to have been described as the Versailles of Morocco. The

Above and opposite: The Foundouq Nejjarin has been restored as part of UNESCO's programme of renovation for Fès. It contains a wealth of woodcarving, with a rich variety of elaborate motifs.

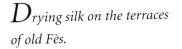
*D*rying silk on the terraces of old Fès.

city is set on two plateaux, separated by the Boukefrane river, and is almost two separate entities. The newer half occupies the right bank of the river, and has a notably regular and orderly layout. The other, on the left bank, consists of the famous imperial city and the medina. It is justly famed for its extraordinary 22 kilometres (14 miles) of ramparts, and for its monumental gates, impressive ruined palace and barracks, and flower-filled gardens. It seems almost another world, on a completely different scale to its surroundings. Meknès was founded in the ninth century by the Zanata Berbers, the descendants of a great Berber tribe, the Meknassa. They settled on this fertile plain with its abundant water, and called their town Meknassa ez-Zeitoun, Meknès of the olive trees. Until the end of the seventeenth century, the town developed only slowly, overshadowed by the great imperial city of Fès. But from that point onwards, the town was totally transformed by one man: the redoubtable Alawi sultan Moulay Ismail who, distrusting the rebellious people of Fès and the crafty inhabitants of Marrakesh, made Meknès the centre of his kingdom. The sultan carried out a huge amount of

Every inch of space in the crowded medina is used, including the rooftops. Here, tanners use them for drying hides.

construction during his fifty-five-year reign from 1672 to 1727. Although the complex of buildings which formed his palace is now either completely destroyed or in ruins, some of the remains – such as the underground royal granary – give an indication of the vast size of this former imperial city. Some distance away are traces of what is believed to have been a stable, large enough to accommodate the sultan's 12,000 horses. Towards the south, the sultan's grandson Sidi Mohamed Ben Abdallah built a huge castle, the Dar el-Beida, which is now a renowned military academy.

The gates of Meknès are one of its major attractions, and the huge entrance to the medina is particularly impressive. The Bab el-Berdain, the gate on the northern side of the medina, is monumental in its proportions, while the Bab el-Khemis, to the west, is extraordinarily richly decorated. Another gate, the Bab Moulay Ismail, leads into the mausoleum of Moulay Ismail; here again, a masterpiece of Islamic art commemorates the sultan who was piously revered by the Moroccans.

Fès is an important focal point for communications between the

*T*he hill town of Moulay Idriss is a very important holy place.

• Moulay Idriss and its moussem •

The town of Moulay Idriss lies to the north of Meknès, overlooking the ruins of the Roman city of Volubilis. It is Morocco's most important place of pilgrimage. Each year, religious fraternities and pilgrims from all over the country assemble at the mausoleum of Moulay Idriss, the founder of the first Islamic kingdom in western North Africa. The many festivities held to commemorate this great religious event are known collectively as the moussem. One of the high points of the moussem is a ceremony in which horsemen in traditional costume, each representing a particular tribe, gallop along together firing shots into the air with their mokalhas, the long rifles with inlaid decoration which have been in use since the seventeenth century. But the most impressive moment occurs on the Friday evening and continues throughout the night: the participants pray and work themselves into a state of increasing spiritual intoxication, culminating in an extraordinary trance which, they believe, expiates their sins.

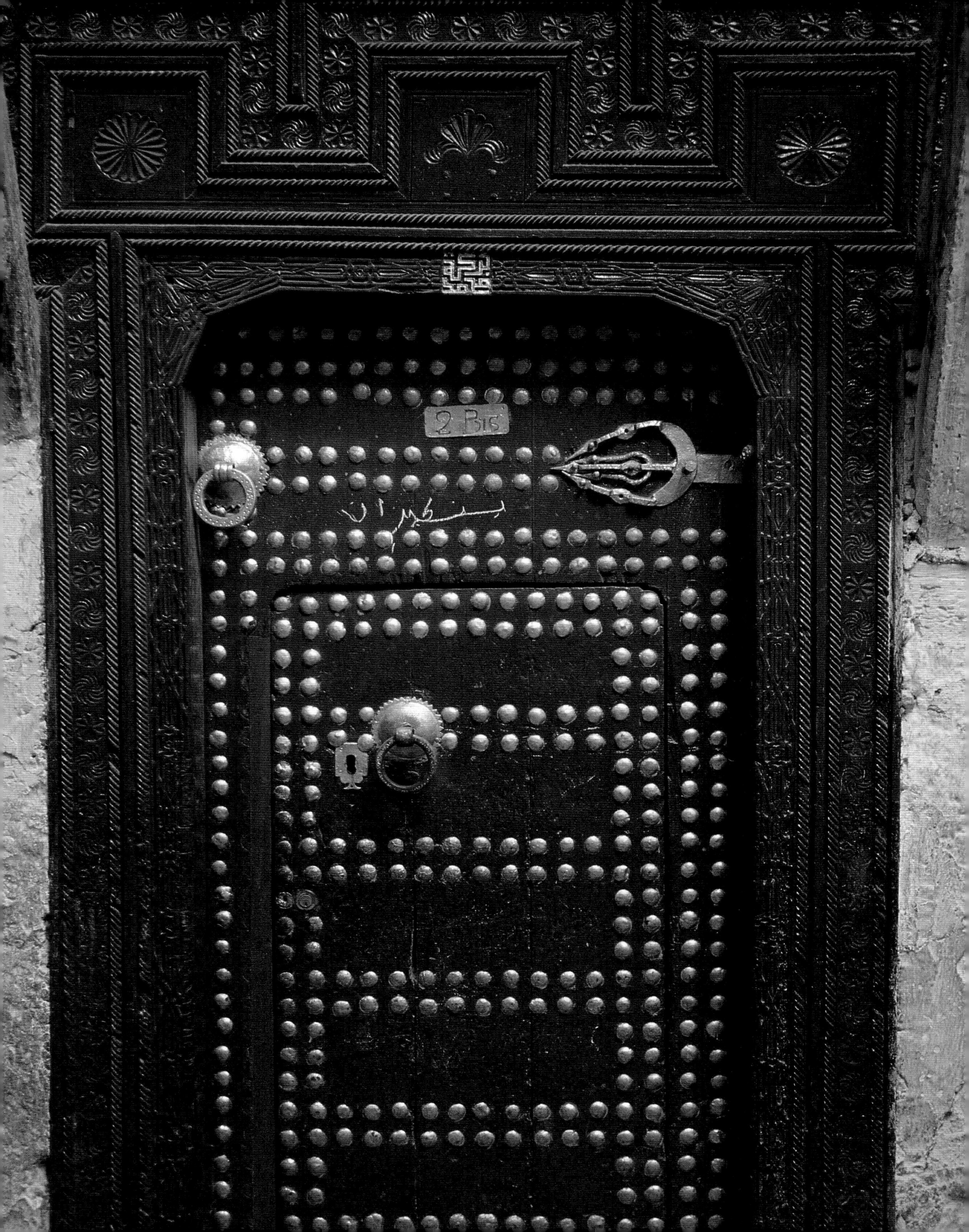
2 Bis

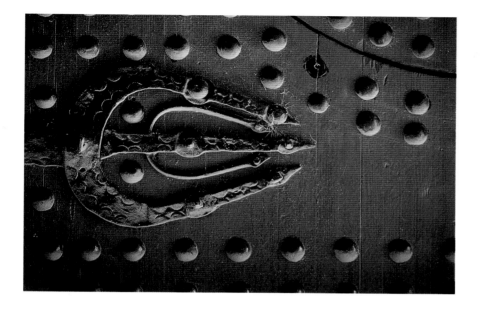

In Morocco, the humble front door is often a work of art in its own right.
Overleaf: The ruins of Volubilis are now an open-air museum, and a reminder of the Roman presence in ancient times. The heart of the city was the forum, surrounded by the Capitol, a triumphal arch, baths, and houses.

Mediterranean and black Africa, and between the Atlantic and the eastern part of North Africa.

It is also the intellectual and religious centre of Morocco; set like a jewel within its ramparts, Fès is undoubtedly the most precious of Moroccan cities.

It is also the oldest of the imperial cities, a holy place with a shifting, cosmopolitan population whose influence has extended far and wide during its long history. Far from being a historical monument, it is a living city and a very busy one at that. The famous quarter of Fès el-Bali, for example, is where immigrants from as far afield as Cordoba in Spain and Kairouan in Tunisia settled in the ninth century. The dazzlingly white section of the city known as Fès el-Jedid (New Fès) was built by the Marinids in the thirteenth century. The narrow streets, houses, shops, gardens, and mosques teem with people, and the abundance of foodstuffs and other products from all over Africa and beyond recalls the city's heyday, when caravans laden with spices, silk, and gold halted at this important and popular staging-post. Wheat, beans, citrus fruit, aubergines,

These and following pages: In Chefchaouen, the geometric shapes of the neat cubic houses contrast with the apparently random tangle of the street layout.

The sound of laughter is never far away in Chefchaouen as children play in the winding streets.

meat, fish, and pastries are bought and sold in much the same way as they were in medieval times.

Fès is also the capital of Moroccan craftsmanship. Much of the credit for the extraordinary beauty of its mosques, palaces, medersas (Koranic schools), and fountains lies with its skilful decorative artists, woodcarvers, mosaic-makers, and ceramists. In fact, the artisans of Fès are renowned throughout the Muslim world. The mosaics and zelliges – the wonderful blue, green, white, or black ceramic panels used to decorate floors and walls – are complex and subtle. The ornate, sinuous motifs and overall richness of decoration reflect the Andalusian influence, and the dominant colour, blue, creates a cool, cheerful effect. In every district of the medina (each of which is almost an independent entity) there are masterpieces adhering closely to the traditions of Hispano-Islamic art.

Fès's omnipresent decorative arts are the legacy of generations of sultans with sophisticated tastes. They, too, were responsible for its status as a city of learning and culture, centred on the famous university mosque of Qarawiyin and the city's seven medersas or Koranic

schools. Particularly during the Marinid era, the sultans were deter-mined to make this imperial city a place of intellectual fervour.

So rich and fertile was this tradition of knowledge that it shaped the spirit of Fès for centuries. The city earned a reputation for insub-ordination and rebelliousness which struck fear into the hearts of some of the sultans, just as it did the French when they invaded Morocco. The word *istiklal*, independence, echoed constantly around the walls of the Qarawiyin Mosque during the forty-four years of the French protectorate.

The medersas are places of both heated intellectual debate and cool, measured contemplation. Undoubtedly the most attractive are those of Bu Inanya and Attarine, with their elaborately sculpted wood and mosaics. Bu Inanya is unusual in the way in which it bal-ances the proportions of the different parts of the building, and in its majestic scale. Water is omnipresent here: in the great ablution room, students, market traders, and shop owners purify themselves in basins of water before entering the prayer hall.

Top: The Bab el-Mansour, one of the huge gates of Meknès. Above and opposite: The entrance to the mausoleum of Moulay Ismail.

*A*bove and opposite: The mausoleum of Moulay Ismail.
In the Islamic world, calligraphy is an important art form in its own right,
singing the praises of God and uniting the community of believers.

• The mausoleum of Moulay Ismail •

Sultan Moulay Ismail was much admired by the Moroccans for his fierce independence and his courage as a warrior. His mausoleum consists of two rooms, only one of which non-Muslims are allowed to enter. This square room has a superb domed ceiling supported by twelve columns; the room which is the sultan's final resting-place is larger.

Both rooms are fine examples of the splendour of Islamic art. The beauty of the glazed earthenware tiles in geometric motifs, stucco, and sculpted plaster is a hymn of praise to God and the prophet Mohammed, while the arabesque decorations and calligraphy combine geometric rigour with fantasy of form. This tomb is an awesome expression of the truth and beauty of Islam.

This page: Before the road was built across the Tizi n'Tichka pass, the large village of Telouet, 1,800 metres (5,500 feet) above sea level, was an important transit point for camel caravans.
Opposite and previous pages: The high plains of the Atlas, with Jebel Mgoun on the horizon.

The High Atlas is the gigantic arc of mountains which forms the physical heart of Morocco. It is a natural fortress of jagged peaks, creating a barrier nearly 700 kilometres (450 miles) long in which broad, high valleys alternate with deep canyons. With more than a hundred peaks over 3,500 metres (11,550 ft) in height, this mountain range is still undergoing a complex and active process of geological change. As well as being the source of much of Morocco's water, the High Atlas also forms the demarcation line between the northern part of the country, with its mild oceanic climate, and the southern half with its endless expanses of desert.

Top: The town of Rich.
Above: The kasbah of Tagoundaft, on the Tizi n'Test road.

There are three places where vehicles can cross this great barrier of basalt, limestone, and clay: either via the passes of Tizi n'Test or Tizi n'Tichka, or along the road joining the high plateaux of the Imilchil region to the gorges of the Dadès and Todra watercourses. Large numbers of Berber tribespeople live along this important geographical frontier, for this is the fortress in which they built their civilization. Their world is dominated by the five great peaks of the High Atlas, running from north-east to south-west: Jebel Ayachi, with its forest of cedars; Jebel Mourik, with its high, spreading plateaux; Jebel Mgoun, with its powerful limestone peaks; Jebel Toukbal, the highest of them all; and Jebel Ras Moulay Ali, at the end of this great wall of mountains, not far from Agadir.

The Berbers have maintained their own unique lifestyle, customs, and forms of social organization. They regard themselves as separate from other people and close to God, and farmers and pastoralists alike have imprinted their personality on the hillsides and valleys of this awe-inspiring region. There are many different itineraries you can follow if you wish to meet these independent,

pious, and enigmatic men and women, with their legendary hospitality and generosity. André Fougerolles, who describes many of
them in his famous book about the High Atlas, writes: "There is
an extraordinary network of tracks which are in constant use,
allowing you to design an itinerary to suit your own particular abil-
ities and interests. They are accessible for most of the year, though
in winter and spring you will need to be a mountaineer and a skier
to cope with the region's great peaks and passes. There are an in-
finite number of villages, hamlets, and remote settlements at alti-
tudes of up to 2,400 metres (1,500 ft), with people leading simple
but busy lives, pleasant, and proud…This is a highly attractive world
which still awaits discovery."

This rural environment, which has changed little for generations,
is both fascinating and complex. As well as its great variety of landscapes, there are many different tribes, dialects, and traditions,
though the people can be divided broadly into three groups. The
Beraber, who speak dialects of Tamazirht, are still nomadic or
semi-nomadic.

Winters are harsh in the high plains of the Atlas.

Most of them migrate between the eastern High Atlas, the central Middle Atlas, and the valleys of the Ziz, the Todra, and the Dadès. The Shluh people, who speak various dialects of Tachelhit, are sedentary farmers who have settled in the central and western High Atlas and in the Anti-Atlas. Finally, the Riffi or Riffian people inhabit the Rif and speak Tamazirht. The Berbers are the original inhabitants of Morocco. They came from the Orient and from East Africa, and were Islamicized by the Arab tribes during the invasions of the eighth to twelfth centuries, becoming fervent, proudly independent Muslims and valiant fighters. They engaged in frequent skirmishes over pastures and the transhumance routes along which herds are seasonally moved to the higher mountain grasslands. André Bertrand mentions in his book, *Tribus berbères du Haut Atlas*, that: "Their distinct feature is – or was – the extremely intricate nature of their tribal civilization, which was comparable in its complexity to a carpet made from thousands of little strands. But French pacification blocked their transhumance routes for several years and then deprived the regions of any autonomy they may

Above, opposite, and previous pages: Scenes from the Tichka region.
Overleaf: In places, the Dadès valley bears a striking resemblance to the American wild west.

Above: Dadès. Above right: The Todra Gorge. Top: Boulmane du Dadès.

once have had. This broke the threads of the carpet, and today it is crumbling away, taking with it a very distinctive way of life."

There is visible evidence of this depressing fact in the local homes, each of which was traditionally occupied by all the members of an extended family; nowadays, each houses only a couple and their children. Kasbahs, also commonly known as ksour (ksar in the singular), were the former habitat of the patriarchal Berber society. They are fortified villages with walls made from clay soil moulded between two planks, originally designed to house the extended family, their animals and their crops. The thick, high walls protect those inside from attack, and small slit windows keep the interior cool.

The "road of the thousand kasbahs" passes through the Dadès valley. Despite having been eroded by the wind and rain, they look out across the valley with a proud air.

The architecture is tailored to the needs of a communal existence: kasbahs have several storeys (up to five or six in the case of the more elaborate homes) and reflect the patriarchal hierarchy of Berber society. They are citadels surrounded by ramparts, which may be small or large, and contain a mosque, a public open space, and collective granaries sometimes known as agadir. But although people still live in kasbahs in the Todra and Dadès valleys, and in a few oases in the Sahara, it is increasingly common to see them in ruins, eroded by the wind and abandoned in favour of individual houses.

The tribes are becoming increasingly fragmented, the men no longer devote their lives to waging war, and the nomads are becoming more and more sedentary, but nonetheless the Berbers continue to live in close harmony with nature, following the rhythm of the seasons. The peasants laboriously plough their fields in autumn with a simple hoe, as they have done since ancient times. Winter is the most difficult time of year, for the climate is cold and snowy, and the women sometimes have to go out in search of firewood, which they

carry back in heavy bundles. Spring is the season of fertility when the farmers sow wheat and barley, and the pastoralists leave the valleys and return to their summer grazing. This is also the season when water is most plentiful, as the rivers are swollen with melt-water and can be used to operate watermills and make bread. In summer, the women have to work doubly hard, for as well as maintaining the home they have to bring in the harvest. During this season, the clear mountain air is filled with the invigorating fragrance of rosemary and arbutus, or cane-apple. In the central and western High Atlas, the mountains and valleys are covered in greenery: juniper, Aleppo pines, evergreen oaks, and walnut trees, with the Moroccan timber tree known as the argan further to the west.

Each week, the men are given a brief respite from the workaday routine in the form of a visit to the souk, the weekly market, to buy and sell produce.

The souk is a major meeting-place for all the local Berbers, an excuse to meet up with friends, haggle, and catch up on the latest gossip. Around them, the donkeys and mules which are the main

The Dadès river is lined with fields, orchards, palm trees, and rose bushes.

This and opposite pages: Tinerhir is a small, prosperous town surrounded by one of the most beautiful palm groves in southern Morocco.

form of transport for the men and their produce wait patiently until their owners return.

The period from July to September, when work in the fields is finished, is a time for festivals. These take place all over the Atlas region, and are important for a number of reasons. Firstly, they are an occasion for celebration, lasting several days and involving large numbers of villagers from all over the region. They are also an opportunity for families to form alliances by marrying off their children, and in fact the festival season is closely associated with wedding celebrations. For several days the high plateaux, the valleys, and the mountainsides echo with the sound of music, singing, and hand-clapping.

This page: The Tissint region is known for its fine silver jewellery and elaborately coloured clothes. Opposite page: Berber woman from the Atlas mountains.

*J*ewellery plays an important part in the lives of the Berbers. There is a proverb that says: "If you wish to be beautiful, you must allow your ears to be pierced."

As a form of ritual, dancing is closely bound up with music, singing, and poetry. The main form of dance music is called ahouach. The men play drums on frames, held in one hand and struck with the other, along with other drums shaped like goblets, and flutes. Singers intone melodious, poetic songs to the fiery music, and the beautifully dressed women dance in a circle. On feast-days, they pay particular attention to their hair, make-up, and silver jewellery. The way in which they plait their hair with pieces of coloured wool shows which tribe they belong to, while their make-up and tattoos are used partly as a form of facial decoration, and partly to show their tribal allegiance and protect them from the evil eye.

The town of Imilchil is the administrative centre of the Ait Hadiddou tribe, who live on the high plateaux. It is also the venue for one of Morocco's most famous annual events, known as the moussem, or festival. It is also called the "fair of the fiancés", involves hundreds of people, and lasts for several days.

The fact that this festival is so famous, and so successful in helping people to find partners, is due at least in part to the atmosphere

*M*any Berber men carry daggers, some of them made from beautifully tooled silver.

of magic which surrounds the venue. The two large lakes near the festival site, Isli and Tisli, have traditionally been regarded by the Berbers as symbols of love. According to legend, a very long time ago, a young man and a young woman fell head over heels in love, but their families refused to allow them to marry. They wept so copiously that their tears formed these two melancholy-looking lakes.

As though to celebrate and perpetuate this myth, the Ait Hadiddou organize this festival, which is an opportunity to buy and sell animals, fabrics, and grain, as well as to meet the opposite sex with a view to marriage. Unusually, it is the men who do the parading as potential suitors, and the women – girls, widows, and divorcees – who do the choosing. For hours on end, the musicians beat their drums in accompaniment to slow, swaying dances. At the closing ceremony the couples who have been married by the doul (notary) dance the ahaidous and sing love songs.

To the south of Morocco lies the great Sahara, where the country's African roots are most apparent. The landscape in this spectacular region of oases and countless kasbahs is full of contrasts, and anything but monotonous. Islands of palm groves, green and fertile riverbanks, and fields of cultivated roses are dwarfed by an ocean of rocky plateaux and sand whipped by the hot wind.

Tafilalet is everyone's idea of what a cool oasis should look like. Located between Er Rachidia – the regional capital and the cradle of the Alawi dynasty – and Erfoud, the Ziz valley snakes its way through the desert, with hundreds of thousands of date palms flourishing alongside.

This spectacular river of greenery has been called the Mesopotamia of North Africa. Located in a strategic position for trading links between black Africa and the north of the continent, Tafilalet has played a key role in Morocco's economic development. It was an essential stopping-point for caravans from the Sahara, and attracted merchants from the big commercial cities such as Fès, Tlemcen,

The kasbah of Ait Benhaddou, near Ouarzazate, is a UNESCO World Heritage Site.

and even Cairo, who came to sell products which would end up in the big cities of sub-Saharan Africa. Sijilmassa, today a small collection of ruins, was the powerful capital of the Tafilalet region in the Middle Ages, and the point on which this large volume of caravan traffic converged. After Erfoud, as you descend towards Merzouga, comes the first in an endless series of sand dunes, providing a reminder of how incredibly difficult and dangerous the desert crossing used to be. Confronted with this ever-changing landscape, which to the outsider seems a harsh, strange place, the visitor is made fully aware of the Africanness of southern Morocco. Towards the west, as you pass alongside Jebel Sahro, is the small and prosperous town of Tinerhir, surrounded by one of the most beautiful palm groves in the south of the country. The town is the crossing-point between the High Atlas and Jebel Sahro, and overlooks the entrance to the deep, narrow Todra gorge, with cliffs 300 metres (1,000 ft) high on either side, and the beginning of the famous "road of the thousand kasbahs". Set amid the arid, rocky foothills of the Atlas and the fertile palm groves, Tinerhir blends

*T*op: *The kasbah of Tiffoultout, near Ouarzazate, marks the entrance to the Drâa valley.*
Left: The Ziz valley.
Above: The entrance to the kasbah of Ait Benhaddou.
Overleaf: The huge lake created by the El Mansour Ed-Dahbi Dam, near Ouarzazate.

Taourirt kasbah, near Ouarzazate, is a major tourist attraction.

into the landscape, but its cubic pink and earth-coloured houses stand out starkly against the deep blue sky.

As you continue along the kasbah road towards Ouarzazate, you discover the gorges of the Dadès river, a place of powerful natural beauty. Amid the majestic folds of rock, sculpted by erosion and varying in colour from red to mauve, the kasbahs, made from the same multicoloured earth, seem almost to be an organic part of the soil itself. After Boulmane-du-Dadès, which marks the beginning of this unforgettable landscape, the road reaches El Kelaa M'Gouna, which is famous for its distilleries where roses are made into perfume. Together with the splendour of the kasbahs and the beauty of the landscape with its hills and valleys, thousands of rose bushes provide an additional splash of colour in a succession of fields and orchards. Their heady fragrance accentuates the sense of freedom, a feeling which grows as this fast road winds its way towards Ouarzazate. A constant succession of kasbahs is set against a background of greenery: Dar Ait Souss, Dar Aichil, el-Kabbaba, and Amerhidil, hidden away amid the vast palm grove of Skoura.

*F*int oasis.

This luxuriant oasis, with its countless rose bushes and almond, apple, and cherry trees, was founded in the twelfth century by Yacoub el-Mansour. It marks the end of the Dadès valley, and is dominated by Jebel Mgoun. Forty kilometres (25 miles) further on, after having crossed a more arid area and passed the lake created by the dam at Al-Mansour Ed-Dahbi, you reach the important town of Ouarzazate, built as a garrison in 1928 for strategic reasons. It is a gateway to the vast expanses of the south, at the crossing of the roads leading to Agadir, Marrakesh, and the Dadès and Drâa valleys. Today, it is a major regional economic centre, with a large number of pink-painted shops, open-air markets, and little craft workshops. Traders and farmers from the surrounding countryside come here to do business. The goods on display include rosewater and musk, henna, cumin, ginger, and paprika, as well as ouzguita carpets with their symbolic blue and gold geometric motifs, silver jewellery, and coloured fabrics.

Ouarzazate is an important tourist centre, with plenty of hotels. Its dry, harsh, and vividly coloured landscape has also been a major

*T*he village of Adai, near Tafraoute.

• Tafraoute •

The superb little town of Tafraoute sits in a valley 1,200 metres (4,000 ft) up in the mountains of the Anti-Atlas, surrounded by pink granite hills. Huge blocks of eroded stone have tumbled down the hillsides, creating a lunar landscape which looks as though it has been rocked by an earthquake or a shower of meteorites; in some cases these actually lean against the pink and red walls of the buildings. Palms and almond trees soften the beauty of the landscape, and in early spring, when the almond trees are covered in pink and white blossom, this little valley is truly a sight for sore eyes. The light plays on the rocks and trees, bringing out their colours in magnificent shades of red, ochre, and mauve. Every local Shluh Berber dreams of setting up a shop or a business in one of the northern cities, making his fortune, and then coming back, buying a piece of land, and building a house on it.

Around Tafraoute, there are many villages perched on the rocky hillsides.

draw for film-makers: movies made here include *Lawrence of Arabia* and *The Last Temptation of Christ*. The town is also a popular destination for people from Casablanca, who come here for a few days of rest and relaxation if they have the time and the money. One must-see is the Kasbah Taourirt, a citadel built by the Glaoui, the last of Marrakesh's redoubtable pashas. Its high, delicately sculpted ochre-coloured walls of dried mud, crenellated towers, and façades dotted with small windows create a complex, interwoven pattern. Inside, the apartments have retained their superb sculpted cedarwood ceilings, and sometimes a stork's nest adds a touch of movement to an otherwise still and uninhabited building.

The fortified village of Ait Benhaddou, 20 kilometres (13 miles) out of Ouarzazate on the road to Marrakesh, is one of Morocco's most famous kasbahs. It has been designated a World Heritage Site by UNESCO, and attracts a growing number of admiring visitors to its mountainside eyrie. The large multistorey houses match the rock of the mountain so closely that they appear almost to have grown out of it, and the small number of palms and almond trees

seem to have been deliberately planted to enhance the effect of this extraordinary arrangement of stone.

Village near Tafraoute.

From Ouarzazate to Mhamid, on the Algerian border, the Oued Drâa river creates a 200-kilometre (125-mile) ribbon-like oasis, carpeting the surrounding area with greenery. The river defies the desert and dispenses its bounty across the valley, a tiny trickle compared to the vastness of the great red sand-dunes. Eventually, it flows into the ocean over a thousand kilometres (six hundred miles) away. In 1884, Charles de Foucault wrote in his book, *Reconnaissance au Maroc*: "Along the banks of the Oued Drâa, the valley floor is like an enchanted garden, crowded with fig and pomegranate trees whose leaves intertwine to create deep shadow on the ground beneath.

The tall plumes of palm-trees are poised above them… Everywhere, there are indications of an affluent population: cereals and vegetables growing beneath palms and fruit trees, vine-covered arbours, pavilions made of dried mud providing places of cool shade and repose where the people can spend the hot hours of the day…

Right: In February, the countryside around Tafraoute comes alive with pink and white almond blossom. Opposite: One of the square red minarets which are a typical feature of the Tafraoute region.

Countless ksour are ranged along the lower slopes on either side of the river, though few have been built on the valley floor, partly to maximize the amount of precious soil available, and partly because of fear of flooding. All share the same elegance which is particular to buildings along the Drâa: every wall is covered in ornamental mouldings and designs, and whitewashed crenellations ... Even the poorest houses are decorated with pinnacle turrets, rows of arches, and open balustrades."

Along the road to Zagora, a large village on the edge of the Sahara desert, palms bend under the weight of yellow dates, and cultivated fields are rich in pink laurels, acacias, orange, lemon, and almond trees, vegetables, and cereals – not at all what you would expect in such an arid region.

Above: The pavilion of Menara, surrounded by olive groves and the snow-capped peaks of the Atlas. Opposite page: The walls of the town of Tiznit, between Tafraoute and Agadir.

Marrakesh, the capital of southern Morocco, is one of the jewels in the country's crown. Sprawled across the plain of Haouz and surrounded by green palm groves, it is like a red pearl nestling beneath the snow-capped peaks of the Atlas mountains. This illustrious city exerts a magic of its own even when viewed from afar. As you approach it from the north, the flat, dry, spreading plain is in stark contrast to the grandeur of the High Atlas mountains, immense, massive, sheer, and apparently inaccessible. Then, the welcoming green fronds of palm trees offer a foretaste of the verdancy to come.

Once you have crossed the Oued Tensift, the first gateway to Marrakesh, you see the city itself, its deep orange-red walls providing a reminder that the desert is never very far away here. The impression that you are entering an oasis on the edge of a very different world from that of northern Morocco is heightened by the heat, for Marrakesh has a drier and harsher climate than that of the north. This is a hot, energetic, bustling city.

The long Avenue Mohamed V is the main link between the old city

(with its great medina, the famous Djemaa el-Fna square, and its kasbah and palaces) and the new town, represented by the Gueliz district. The avenue is vibrant from morning to night, and typifies the tireless energy of Marrakesh; being a major traffic route, it is clogged with cars, mopeds, bicycles, and traditional carriages wending their way in all directions. Also, it is an important meeting-place for the young people of Marrakesh, who are very westernized. The young men and women who meet here, between the Place du 16 Novembre and the Place Abd el-Moumin Benali, discuss whatever comes to mind and flirt with one another in complete disregard of the Muslim ban on women flaunting themselves in this way. These pioneers of a new generation provide an opportunity to appreciate the extraordinary sensual beauty of the women of Marrakesh. They have traditionally been compared to gazelles, and you can see why when you look at their oval faces, large, round black eyes, and prominent eyebrows.

As they look at you, their gaze is penetrating, proud, and yet brief and fleeting as though the old admonitions about eye contact still

The cobalt blue of Majorelle contrasts with the luxuriant greenery of the garden which surrounds it.

*S*pices are sold everywhere in Morocco,
and are widely used in its cuisine.

• Tajine of lamb with prunes •

A delicious, fragrant, and colourful stew, with a subtle combination of sweet and savoury flavours. Serves four.

Ingredients: 1 kg (2 lb) of lamb, a handful of prunes, two onions, two knobs of butter, a pinch each of saffron and cinnamon, three dessertspoons of honey, a few almonds, two dessertspoons of oil, salt and pepper to taste.

Heat the oil in a casserole dish and brown the meat and the onions. Add the butter, saffron, salt, and pepper. Then add one cup of water and simmer over a low heat for about an hour. Remove the meat, and add the prunes, cinnamon, and honey. Simmer for fifteen minutes, and then mix in the meat again. Serve immediately, preferably on a tajine dish and garnish with almonds.

have not worn off completely. Although they no longer bother to hide their beauty, you feel there is still a side to them that will remain forever enigmatic, hidden away like the faces of their mothers and grandmothers.

This feeling of heady oriental sensuality is heightened as you continue along the Avenue Mohamed V to the Djemaa el-Fna. This square is the main focal point and palpitating heart of Marrakesh. Glowing beneath a blue sky, it has many different faces at different times of day, but is particularly unforgettable in the early evening as the sun falls. Perhaps one of the best vantage points from which to watch the sunset is one of the balcony restaurants in the hotels overlooking the square. This magnificent spectacle bathes the sky and the city in fire, and the square gradually fills with people as the magic hour approaches.

Eventually, it is seething with humanity as crowds of fifty to a hundred people form motionless circles around the musicians, dancers, and stallholders, lost in fascination as other people flow around them. Pedestrians, bicycles, mopeds, carts, and small taxis hurry

The art of dyeing cloth in brilliant colours has been passed down for countless generations.

*T*op: *Marrakesh is known as "the city of roses".*
Above and right: The countless craftsmen and women working in the souk are justifiably proud of their skills, and offer a warm welcome to visitors.

in and out of the medina of which the Djemaa el-Fna is an exten-sion, and there is a feeling of constant motion. The air is filled with the noise of trumpets, tambourines, the bells which water carriers use to attract attention, screeching birds, radios, car horns, and hand-clapping, creating an extraordinary and unforgettable cacophony. The crowds from the souks in the medina overflow into the square, and a battalion of orange-juice sellers divides it into two separate halves. As evening descends, a brilliant yellow-orange halo forms around the sun, and a dazzling light starts to turn the flat roofs of the city into an indistinguishable blur. Darkness begins to set in, and the first electric lights and oil lamps are lit. The blue of the sky is gradually replaced by a pink and yellow haze, and the sun becomes an enormous ball of fire which descends so rapidly you think you can almost see it moving.

A few fleeting clouds form wispy patterns in the sky, emphasizing the intensity and variety of hues conjured up by the sunset. The luminous bright reds and oranges struggle to survive for a few more moments, before being swallowed up by the gloom; darkness

The Djemaa el-Fna, Marrakesh's central square, bombards the visitor with exotic sights, sounds, and smells.

A rare moment of tranquillity amid the organized chaos of the souk.

descends on the city like an inky-black sandstorm, and the stars take up watch for the night again.

After dark, on the western side of the Djemaa el-Fna, officers from the police headquarters keep a stern eye on the behaviour of the "guides" – young unemployed men offering tours of the medina whether you want them or not. Several rows of food stalls put in an appearance, offering a variety of dishes to whet the appetite: couscous, barbecued meat, vegetable salads, the soup known as harira, and fried fish. The combination of the stallholders' blandishments and the aroma of their cooking is a difficult one to resist. All around them, other groups ply their various trades.

Traditional singers, musicians, and dancers use their art to express aspects of Berber life; these are instantly understood and appreciated by the people of the medina, most of whom are Berbers themselves. Nearby, travelling entertainers perpetuate the tradition of the *gnaoua*, the religious fraternity descended from black Sudanese former slaves, who practise trance and ritual possession. Women fortune-tellers, traders from the Orika valley or the Sahara desert

selling folk remedies, snake-charmers, and water-sellers all enhance the strong sense that everyone in this extraordinary square is part of one huge family. The Djemaa el-Fna is the social hub of the entire city, a chance for the local people to celebrate their membership of the community, earn a livelihood, or simply pass the time of day with friends and acquaintances.

In the morning, as the temperature rises, the square wears a different face. During the day it is a market, buzzing with the same frenetic activity as the souks themselves. The legendary souks of Marrakesh live up to their reputation for being very large and very crowded, but for all the apparent chaos there is a system to them. If you have never been into a souk before, entering one in Marrakesh is an unforgettable rite of passage.

Its long, narrow, winding streets are lined with small shops, divided into areas where particular craftspeople and merchants ply their trades. In one section, textile-makers sell brightly coloured jellabas, veils, rolls of fabric, kaftans, and dresses, some distinctly gaudy and others in muted shades of a single colour. The light in the souk has

*A*bove, right: *Tajines, the covered containers for the stew which is the national dish.*

133

a very distinct quality of its own, soft, dappled, and filtered by the ceilings of wooden trelliswork and reeds, so that one particular object may be dramatically lit and the others around it scarcely visible in the gloom. Carpenters and woodcarvers sell superb pieces sculpted from cedar, walnut, and olivewood, skilfully sawing, chiselling, and planing in the semi-darkness of their windowless shops. Further down the same street are areas devoted to the morocco-leather workers and shoemakers, who churn out vividly coloured oriental-style pouffes, cushions, bags, and slippers, as well as traditional saddles and harnesses. Here, everything in the souk seems to have been imbued with the rich scent of leather since time immemorial. Elsewhere, gold and silversmiths and metalworkers deploy the same skills as their forebears have used for a thousand years or more, their designs combining flowing arabesque forms with strict geometric motifs.

Another craft for which Morocco is renowned is carpet-making. In the carpet quarter, every square inch of wall, floor, and shopfront is draped in designs originating from all over the Arab world, full

This page and opposite: Marrakesh's decorative arts at their sophisticated best.

of warm, bright colours and intricate patterns. At its best, Moroccan craftsmanship follows the precepts of Islamic art, in which the harmony and equilibrium of the spiritual is reflected in everyday, temporal objects. The aesthetic codes and the accumulated wisdom which go into making these products are the expression of an entire way of life. The generous and hospitable welcome afforded by most of the craftspeople in the souk, who nevertheless drive a hard bargain, is a part of the same desire for happiness and harmony as that expressed in the beauty of their products.

The Koutoubia Mosque, whose minaret towers 70 metres (230 ft) above the city, is an architectural masterpiece, living proof of the religious piety and extreme sophistication of the Almohad sultans who built it. The building is visible from all over Marrakesh, a landmark for the people of the medina and the inhabitants of the new town.

The Koutoubia is one of the leading examples of Hispano-Moresque art. Its name means "place of the books", a reference to the manuscript market which once stood outside its walls, and it

The Djemaa el-Fna is Marrakesh's central square, crowded with hundreds of Moroccans day and night.

Right: The ancient skill of falconry is a dying art, practised only by a few people.
Opposite: A cobra sways to the sound of a snake-charmer's music in the Djemaa el-Fna.
Overleaf: Traditional musicians from the Tissint region playing at the national folklore festival.

is a grand and uplifting building, its tall, narrow minaret covered in raised designs and painted decoration. Its rhythmic arabesques, lozenge-shaped tracery, and faience mosaics reflect the light and dazzle the eye, while the mosque's forest of pillars, large domes, and Andalusian-style trefoil arches increase the feeling of majesty and strength.

To the north of this great building are the various districts of the kasbah, including the Saadian Tombs, the Palais el-Badi, and the Dar el-Makhzen, the vast royal palace. The tombs are where the Saadian sultans were buried from 1557 onwards, and are a monument to the importance of this dynasty of sharifs, or descendants of Mohammed, whose two-century reign was a time of great prosperity for Marrakesh. The Palais el-Badi is now in ruins, but it is easy to imagine it in its former splendour.

*T*he leaves of the henna bush are dried and boiled to produce a red dye, which women
use to decorate their hands and feet on special occasions such as weddings and festivals.
This very widespread practice is believed to ward off the evil eye.
Opposite: Dancers from the Imintatoute region at the national folklore festival.

• The Marrakesh Festival •

Each year, during the first two weeks of June, a national folklore festival is held in Marrakesh's
Palais el-Badi. Hundreds of participants from every region of Morocco come to the city to perform,
providing a comprehensive overview of Moroccan folk culture, including singing and many different
kinds of dancing such as the trance dances of the religious fraternity known as the gnaoua, the
group dances of the ahouach and the ahaidous, ballet from the Sahara, and war dances from the
Rif and the High Atlas.

The festival is an opportunity to experience the country's great cultural richness, and is very popular
with the Moroccans themselves, who join in with great enthusiasm. Every day at 5 pm comes the
fantasia, the furious horseback charge which is one of the many rituals that form such an integral
part of Moroccan life.

*B*elow, opposite, and previous pages:
The high point of the moussem is the
fantasia, a ritual in which horsemen in
traditional costume, each representing a
particular tribe, gallop along firing
shots into the air. The long, beautifully
decorated rifles, known as mokalhas,
date back to the seventeenth century.

The palace was built in 1578 by the great Saadian sultan Moulay Ahmed el-Mansour, who had just won an important battle against the Portuguese. It was a magnificent building designed to receive guests, but was ruined after the Alawi sultan Moulay Ismail ordered its demolition in 1696. Until then, it had been a dazzling composition in white marble, coloured mosaics, stucco, precious woods, and gold. The austere beauty of this area contrasts with the luxuriant greenery of the gardens in the new town, such as Ménara, Majorelle, and Agdal, which provide their own little oases of tranquillity and coolness in the heat of the noonday sun.

USEFUL INFORMATION

INFORMATION BUREAU: Moroccan Tourist Office,
205 Regent Street, London W1R 7DE, tel. 0171 437 0073.

TRAVEL AGENCIES IN MOROCCO: The Moroccan State
Tourist Office has branches all over the country:
22 avenue d'Alger, Rabat, tel. 002127-730562,
fax 002127-727917; Immeuble A, place du Prince
Héritier Sidi Mohamed, Agadir, tel. 002127-
846377, fax 002127-846378; 55 rue
Omar Slaoui, Casablanca, tel. 002127-
271177; Place Abdelmoumen Ben Ali,
Marrakesh,
tel. 002127-436131, fax 002127-436057;
29 boulevard Pasteur, Tangiers,
tel. 002127-948661, fax 002127-948050.

ENTRY FORMALITIES: A valid passport is
all you need; Europeans are not asked to
produce a visa or an inoculation
certificate. On entering the country you
will have to fill in a *carte d'embarcation*,
which among other information asks
for an address. If you are driving you
must have your car papers and a green insurance card for
Morocco with you. Cars are entered in your passport when you
come into the country.

MOROCCAN EMBASSY: Moroccan Embassy, 49 Queens Gate
Gardens, London SW7 5NE, tel. 0171 581 5001.

BRITISH EMBASSY IN MOROCCO: 17 boulevard Saomaat Hassan,
BP 45, Rabat, tel. 002127-720906.

HEALTH AND INOCULATIONS: Prophylactic treatment against malaria is not necessary. Inoculations against tetanus and polio are recommended. Check on the current situation with your doctor before you go.

MONEY: The Moroccan unit of currency is the dirham (DH). The exchange rate with the pound sterling in November 1997 was 15 dirhams to £1. There are 100 centimes to one dirham. Coins come in denominations of 5, 10, 20 and 50 centimes, and there are notes worth 10, 50, 100 and 200 dirhams. There are no limits on the importation of foreign currency, though amounts of over 5,000 dirhams must be declared. Credit-card cash advances and traveller's cheque encashments are available from most banks, and credit cards and traveller's cheques are widely accepted in larger hotels, shops, and restaurants.

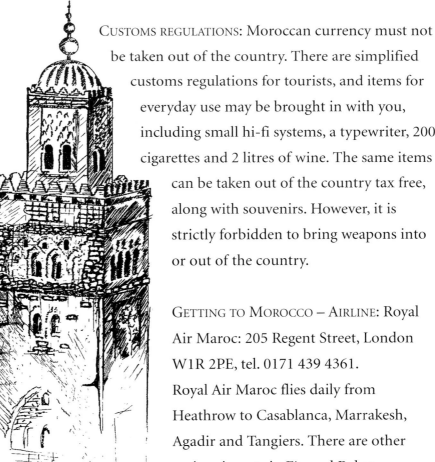

CUSTOMS REGULATIONS: Moroccan currency must not be taken out of the country. There are simplified customs regulations for tourists, and items for everyday use may be brought in with you, including small hi-fi systems, a typewriter, 200 cigarettes and 2 litres of wine. The same items can be taken out of the country tax free, along with souvenirs. However, it is strictly forbidden to bring weapons into or out of the country.

GETTING TO MOROCCO – AIRLINE: Royal Air Maroc: 205 Regent Street, London W1R 2PE, tel. 0171 439 4361. Royal Air Maroc flies daily from Heathrow to Casablanca, Marrakesh, Agadir and Tangiers. There are other major airports in Fès and Rabat.

THE COUNTRY
AND THE PEOPLE

GEOGRAPHY: Morocco is in the north-
west corner of Africa, just south of the
Straits of Gibraltar. It is about 1,600
kilometres (1,000 miles) from Britain. The
country's Atlantic seaboard is about 2,400
kilometres (1,490 miles) in length, and the
Mediterranean coast about 500 kilometres
(300 miles) long. The bordering states are Mauritania
and Algeria.

Cultivated coastal plains and river valleys alternate with
plateaux, rising first to high, thickly forested mountain
ranges, then slowly turning into highland steppes. In
the far south there are sand dunes, the Hamada desert,
and oases where dates are cultivated. The Rif mountains with
their highest peak, Djbel Tidiquin (2,448 metres; 8,031 feet),
run along the Mediterranean coast. The Atlas mountains,
towering above the whole region, divide Morocco into the fertile
north-west and the dry, desert country of the south-east. The
highest peak is Mount Toubkal (4,167 metres; 13,671 feet).

SURFACE AREA: 485,730 km² (157,951 square miles, about twice
the size of Great Britain), together with 252, 120 km² (97,317
square miles) of the Western Sahara area annexed by Morocco
and regarded as an "integral" part of the country.

CAPITAL: Rabat (since 1912), with a population of 1.4 million.

FORM OF GOVERNMENT: Constitutional monarchy.
King Hassan II has ruled the country since 1961.

ECONOMY: The main exports are phosphates, citrus fruits, textiles, olive oil, dates and canned fish. Morocco is the largest phosphates exporter in the world, and one of the major producers of canned sardines. Agadir is the biggest sardine fishing port in the world. Tourism is another important factor in the Moroccan economy.

CLIMATE: The nucleus of Morocco, like southern Europe, lies in a moderate sub-tropical climatic zone. The interior of the country has a continental climate, and because of its mountain ranges is subject to considerable climatic fluctuation, with hot summers and cold winters. In the south the transition to a desert climate begins. Journeys to southern Morocco (Agadir, Marrakesh and the outlying desert areas) are best undertaken in winter. Spring and autumn are the best times for a sightseeing tour of the countryside, and the spring blossom in the north is particularly attractive. It is pleasant on the Atlantic coast and in the mountains in high summer, and as a rule you can bathe in the sea off the southern Atlantic coast all year round.

LOCAL TIME: GMT.

POPULATION: At the turn of the century, the population of Morocco was estimated at four million. Since then, it has been growing dramatically. The 1936 census figure was 5.9 million; by the 1971 census it had risen to 15.4 million, and in September 1994 it stood at no less than 27 million. This growth has meant that the average age is much lower than it used to be; half the people of Morocco are now under 15. A good 50% of the population live in towns, while the other half, the Berbers, live mainly in the country. The only large Moroccan city with a majority Berber population is Marrakesh. Modern Morocco has the largest Jewish community (about 10,000 people) living in any Arab country. The Haratin, descendants of black slaves forcibly brought from West Africa in the sixteenth century and afterwards, live mainly in the oasis regions of southern Morocco.

RELIGION: 99% of the population are Sunni Muslims. Islam is the state religion. There are Jewish and Christian minorities. During the month of the Ramadan fast (beginning on 2 January in 1998) Muslims may neither eat nor drink during daylight hours, and public life comes almost to a standstill. Meals are taken between sunset and sunrise during Ramadan, and are particularly lavish.

LANGUAGE: Arabic is the official language of the country, but there are also several Arabic dialects and the Tamazight spoken by the Berbers. French has been used for international relations, education and trade since the colonial period. Foreign languages spoken are English, Spanish and German.

TOURIST ATTRACTIONS: CASABLANCA is a busy economic centre with 2.7 million inhabitants. The Grande Mosquée Hassan II, built by the king of Morocco as a monument to himself, has become a tourist attraction. It is a vast sacred building, which exerts a magical fascination on believers and tourists from all over the world, and is the only mosque that non-Muslims may enter.

The picturesque town of CHEFCHAOUEN in the Rif mountains is well worth a visit.

Portuguese cisterns were discovered in 1917 in the provincial capital of EL JADIDA, and are the only

remaining trace of former
Portuguese occupation.
FÈS is the oldest of the
four royal cities of
Morocco, and the
richest in art treasures
and architectural
monuments. It was once
the spiritual and political

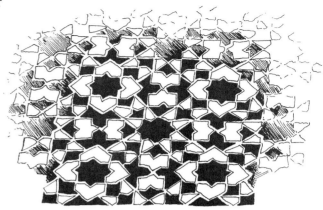

centre of Islam, and until 1912 was the capital of the country.
The Old Town of FÈS EL-BALI has been included in the UNESCO
register of international cultural heritage.

MARRAKESH is one of the most fascinating of Moroccan cities,
and is well worth a visit. The souks of the MEDINA of Marrakesh
are interesting, as is the PLACE JEMAA EL-FNA, which functions as a
market place in the mornings, and in the afternoons becomes a
huge stage for theatrical performances, with jugglers, fire-eaters,
snake charmers and other entertainers displaying their skills.
Being centrally situated, most sightseeing tours of the city begin
in this square.

The fortress city of MEKNÈS, with its imposing town walls almost
20 kilometres (12 ½ miles) in length, lies on the northern spur of
the central Atlas. It has one of the finest funerary mosques in the
country, the MOULAY ISMAEL MOSQUE. Close by, you will find
MOULAY IDRISS, a place of pilgrimage, and the ruins of the
Roman city of Volubilis, now standing among olive groves.

The main sights of RABAT are the OUDAYAS CASBAH and the
NECROPOLIS and MAUSOLEUM OF MOHAMMED V.

You should also try to get up into the ATLAS MOUNTAINS to see
DADES VALLEY, the STREET OF THE THOUSAND CASBAHS, and the
fortified village of Aet-Benhaddou near OUARZAZATE, with its
interlinked casbahs.

In addition, many festivals and religious celebrations are held in
Morocco throughout the year.

These include the almond blossom festival held in Tafraoute in

February; the rose festival at El Kelaâ M'Gouna in May; the wax-palm festival at Salé in May; the national folklore festival in Marrakesh in June; the cherry festival at Séfrou in June; the Desert Symphony at Ouarzazate in June; the camel festival at Guelmin in July; the cultural festival at Asilah in August; the festival of the fiancés at Imilchil in September; the horse festival at Tissa in September; the date festival at Erfoud in October; and the olive festival at Rafsai in December.

INTERNAL TRANSPORT IN MOROCCO: Internal flights in Morocco are plentiful and reasonably priced. Royal Air Maroc offers connecting flights for tourists visiting Morocco. The train services are very good too. Trains run every hour between Rabat and Casablanca, with a journey time of an hour. Other connections with Casablanca run to and from Tangiers, Marrakesh and Meknès. Meknès also has connections to Tangiers and Oujda. A bus journey is the ideal way to see Morocco; there are frequent buses even to remote areas, usually running on time. Many private bus companies compete with the state-run CTM-LN. An alternative to the bus is the *taxi-collectif* or communal taxi service found in many places. Hire cars are very expensive in Morocco, and hard bargaining is advisable, since prices differ a great deal.

MOROCCAN CUISINE: Moroccan cuisine is very sophisticated, with many varieties of vegetables, fish and spices. The national dish is tajine, a stew made of meat, poultry or fish with braised vegetables, olives, almonds, and prunes or preserved lemons. Couscous is the culinary speciality of the Maghreb, and is made of durum wheat semolina served with meat, vegetables and a piquant sauce. It is the traditional dish for the family meal on Friday. Harira is a delicious, thick lamb soup. Méchoui, mutton cooked in the oven or on the spit, is a delicacy for special occasions. Kebabs of beef or chicken are sold from street stalls and in market places. Kesra is the wholemeal bread eaten with all meals, and the repast is often rounded off with succulent pastries containing almonds, honey, and argan-seed oil. The national drink of Morocco is mint tea (*thé à la menthe*), a combination of green China tea and fresh mint, usually heavily sweetened. Fresh fruit juices make a refreshing drink, but you should be sure no water has been added. Mineral water should be drunk only from bottles with crown caps. Alcohol is forbidden to devout Muslims, but it can be bought in tourist centres, large hotels and top restaurants.

Although all information was carefully checked at the time of going to press (November 1997), the publisher cannot accept any responsibility for its accuracy.